b7

Carmen El ati

When I Dance

POEMS BY

James Berry

ILLUSTRATED BY

Karen Barbour

When I Dance

Harcourt Brace Jovanovich, Publishers

SAN DIEGO   NEW YORK   LONDON

First published in Great Britain 1988 by Hamish Hamilton Children's Books

Text copyright © 1991, 1988 by James Berry
Illustrations copyright © 1991 by Karen Barbour

Library of Congress Cataloging-in-Publication Data
Berry, James.
When I dance: poems/by James Berry; illustrated by Karen Barbour.
p.   cm.
Summary: A collection of fifty-nine poems for young adults,
celebrating life in inner-city Britain and in the rural Caribbean.
ISBN 0-15-295568-2
1. Caribbean Area — Juvenile poetry. 2. West Indians — Great
Britain — Juvenile poetry. 3. Young adult poetry, Jamaican.
[1. Caribbean Area — Poetry. 2. West Indians — Great Britain — Poetry.
3. Jamaican poetry.] I. Barbour, Karen, ill. II. Title.
PR9265.9.B47W4   1991
821 — dc20   89-29361

Printed in the United States of America

First United States edition
A B C D E

For
JOANNA

ACKNOWLEDGMENTS

Some of these poems were published in *Poetry Review*, *English in Education* (NATE), *Bluefoot Traveller*, *News for Babylon*, *ILEA Caribbean Anthology*, *I Like That Stuff*, *New Angles*, *Island of the Children*, and *Black Poetry*.

SOURCES OF PROVERBS

Originally Africa, European influences, Caribbean experience, my memory, friends, and the thankful guidance of *Jamaica Proverbs and Sayings* by Izett Anderson and Frank Cundell, published by Irish University Press, Shannon, Ireland.

Contents

ONE

BARRIERS

9

Introduction

These poems draw experience from the inner-city life of Britain and from the rural Caribbean. Their celebrations happen in youth activity. Yet just as they show the joy in dance they also grieve over hurt. They touch dreamlike ways and baffling feelings of aloneness. Impersonal nature grabs us with its violence, overwhelms us with its big giving and exhibits to us its delicate and fantastic self. Animals talk. Oral traditions come over into print.

The poems reflect two cultures, in texture of experience and voice. Sometimes the content is distinctly British, other times Caribbean; then, also, other times the experiences merge.

Glancing again at this body of writing, I see that it shows change, opportunity, struggle, and old concerns. So the poems could be called scooped bits of the times I've lived in. They could also be seen as my special bagful of obsessions and celebrations.

The poems were written over a period of about five years. They were prompted to meet my needs for models in writers' workshops I conducted with young people. Once I had been stirred again by youth interests and preoccupations—and kept under the influence of workshop sessions and readings—some poems arrived as individuals. Others came from time to time, sometimes with partners, often by surprise. In writing them I shared and learned something of current youth culture. I discovered. I had fun. If the celebration here helps to register black people's presence in Britain and in any way assists with Caribbean links and continuity, justification for the effort would be threefold.

Since Independence, Caribbean people have made new demands on their language. Rapidly increased written use of Caribbean Nation Language (Creole) has brought greater attention to it and given it a new status and recognition. Its traditional use in Caribbean writing along with standard English has increased sharply. These poems naturally reflect Caribbean language-use writing traditions and developments.

I mentioned 'change'. Yet, in the concerns of racial relationships in educational terms, change is by far more tenuous than substantial. It is often still left to adventurous students to tumble on a fresh awareness for themselves. As a boy growing up in the Caribbean I responded to British white people as if all were English. It is since living in England I've come to recognize and enjoy the musically different and distinct speaking voices of the Irish, Welsh and Scots. In a similar kind of uninformed way, some 'best educated' people still talk to me, and respond to me, a black man, as if I've just landed from Mars.

In the past, too few poems were crowned sovereign over all other cultures, experiences and voices. Too few poems were selectively celebrated. We've come to a time of change. And yet, only pockets of inner-city education reflect change in any meaningful direction. Occasionally, without obligation, an unexpected school uses bits of material drawn from black people's culture. In the great majority of the nation's schools, nothing substantial at all about black people appears on the syllabuses.

Yet when we actually look, we see that no single sex, race or culture is complete. None has either complete development for itself or to give to any other people. All peoples find themselves pushed to empathize—pushed to see that in a real appreciation of each other's similarity-with-difference there is a key to our learning, our bonding, our development. To grow up, to widen our consciousness and nullify the drive to exclude, damage and restrict other people because of their natural difference, to share and let varied abundance develop—surely, everybody needs a little bit of everybody.

When one's previously excluded cultural experience becomes naturally and properly included in mainstream learning material, one is bound to feel that something validly human has happened to both oneself and attitudes of the old excluding culture. Steps have been taken, away from pure ethnocentricity, in the direction of the human family—wholeness. There is a relaxing of resistance all round; some real change of heart is seen to have happened; new dimensions have been opened in the learning process for both black and white pupils.

In a school situation, particularly, a rejection shows up when at a glance a white child ignores a book knowing it's not for her or him because the cover is illustrated with the image of black children. It shows up when black children are asked into a separate class for special lessons on black culture, as if they alone need it and alone can benefit from it. The attitude also shows up when a teacher declares, 'I can't read black poetry. Nobody'd expect me to read that.'

It stands out that the 'I-can't-read-black-poetry' statement reaffirms that process of keeping black people's experiences excluded from mainstream literature. But it also means that it's not at all appreciated that—treated with particular rhythm stress, with certain accentuation of word pronunciation and performance verve—a lot of classical English poety can be made to sound like rap or dub—made to sound like black poetry. Similarly, in a reverse way, black poetry can be interpreted with a reading that's completely straight. When it comes to the language it uses Caribbean 'dialect' is English based. A poem in 'Creole', or with a mixture of it, will reveal itself with a little patient examination. In any case, ordinarily, for real enjoyment— whatever the kind of language used—a poem is always asking a newcomer to it to first look at it well, find its way of release, its way of relating with its experience, its way that in a reading it is re-created afresh, as if the reader actually wrote it.

It's not necessary, then, for a non-West Indian speaker to try and read a Caribbean language and rhythm poem with the voice of a Caribbean person. A poem yields itself up when sought honestly with feeling, through its movements, rhythms and meaning. When you read any of the Caribbean language-based poems here, do feel out the rhythms. Feel it re-created. Then express it with your own easy natural voice.

Distinct as it is in its culture-spirit and speech rhythms, the Caribbean voice has been around a long time as part of the English-speaking family. Now, here in its new setting, it offers its mainstream contribution in Black British literature.

James Berry
June 1988

Notes on the Poems

Having some attraction for each other, the poems are grouped together by their related themes.

Some of the poems based on Caribbean oral forms will do more than take only one reader's voice. In the manner of the call-and-response religious participation, in its own way—'Scribbled Notes Picked up and Rewritten Because of Bad Grammer, Bad Spelling, Bad Writing', 'What We Said Sitting Making Fantasies', 'Pair of Hands Against Football', 'Sunny Market Song', 'Digging Sing', 'Me Go a Granny-Yard', '11 Riddle Poems', 'Nativity Play Plan', 'Jamaican Caribbean Proverbs', 'Workings of the Wind'—each one of this group offers itself for individual stanza or section sharing by a group reading aloud.

'Digging Sing' is based on the practice of working to the rhythm of a chanting song. 'Work-sing' was used in Jamaica, instead of 'work-song'. Usually on a Saturday, a large group of village men would come together and give a morning's work to one man. This group help was called 'partner-work'. The wife of the man being worked for would go with her friends, and make breakfast for the men, there on the land. Though it didn't happen all the time, sometimes a man would suddenly lead off with a song—usually a bawdy male-orientated chanting song. Others soon came in with the chorus, till the men were one body of work and song.

'Banana Talk' suggests a bunch of bananas talking about its development and way of life. It praises its great god, the sun. 'Big walks' refers to big banana walks, or big fields. 'Banana yellowgold ... for only men' is to do with a common practice among Jamaican small farmers. A man will wrap a small bunch of bananas and bury it on his land to keep it from rats, birds and insects, for him to eat himself. 'A Different Kind of Sunday' highlights a young Caribbean person in a London church daydreaming, making comparisons between a Sunday in the Caribbean and England. 'It's not a donkey and mule holy day/after they'd bathed in sea at sunrise', refers to a Jamaican village practice, which was taking work animals to the sea, bathing them and giving them a swim, early on Sunday mornings. Boys regarded it as a privilege to go with their fathers and the animals.

'Song of the Sea and People' is about the carrying of a newly dug-out canoe from up in the hills, through the village, down to the sea. As was customary, the conchshell or cowhorn was always blown when anything eventful happened in the village. The poem narrates how a group of men carry the canoe, shoulder high in relays, to the sea.

'Bye Now' develops unstated sentiments in the Jamaican term 'Walk good!' which is said when someone is saying a goodbye. The poem is an accumulation of feelings and unexpressed thoughts.

Since Caribbean Independence, Afro-Caribbean artists use much Africa-inspired imagery in their work. While 'Mek Drum Talk, Man' is an Independence celebration poem, it also celebrates Africa's talking drums and their news-carrying function.

Teach the Making
of Summer

Teach the Making of Summer

Dave. Dear Dave.
I could write a letter
of only *Dear Dave.*
My favourite words echo
and whizz me round the world and back.

Did I tell you that when
we talk on the phone I cover
my other ear
to keep your voice in
so that it goes all round my head
and sinks and drifts all about my body?

Dave. Dear Dave.
I write on big paper
to keep your eyes pouring hungrily
over my naked thoughts.

Did I tell you that
next day after seeing you
my feelings get so turned up
it scares me other fellows might touch them?

Did I tell you that thinking suddenly
of a certain person can make
me gasp or gulp or sigh or make
a whimsical moan of a sound
or just hold on to anything near?

Dave. Dear Dave.
Can we start up a school
to teach the making of summer?
You and me have so much!

Rain clouds are heavy today.
An aeroplane passed was like
a submarine overhead, when
in your eyes
is a smile
to meet kisses.

Dave. Dear Dave.
Now, other things may well get done.
I have prayed today.

Susan

There's a mountain now
I can't climb to you
and you don't try.

I can't see
you, can't touch you,
can't just have
hello bouncing back
from eyes a summer road and sky.

An empty seat on my bike,
in me a desolation,
no fun,
everyone goes on.

I should get drunk
they say, but no
I'll stay sober
to dream.

I'll keep a clear eye
looking
nowhere
everywhere.

Date-beggin Sweet Word Them

Look ow I unexpectid—
big ello unexpectid

like new package at yu door
delivad right at yu door

to mix a lickle talk
with a sweet lickle walk

in a stroll from yu door
a-know we nevva did poor

a-hear the city a-sing
wandaful worl a-galang

with we eye them a smile
everywhere all the while

and we work we new strong curves
roun the bright bright discos

eatin a fruit from each stall
with shoes on or none at all—

so June-June yu goin sey yes
we step out and feel we bes?

a-galang—going along

Seeing Granny

Toothless, she kisses
with fleshly lips
rounded, like mouth
of a bottle, all wet.

She bruises your face
almost, with two
loving tree-root hands.

She makes you sit, fixed.
She then stuffs you
with boiled pudding and lemonade.

She watches you feed
on her food. She milks
you dry of answers
about the goat she gave you.

Listn Big Brodda Dread, Na!

My sista is younga than me.
My sista outsmart five-foot three.
My sista is own car repairer
and yu nah catch me doin judo with her.

I sey I wohn get a complex.
I wohn get a complex.
Then I see the muscles my sista flex.

My sista is tops at disco dance.
My sista is well into self-reliance.
My sista plays guitar and drums
and wahn see her knock back double rums.

I sey I wohn get a complex.
I wohn get a complex.
Then I see the muscles my sista flex.

My sista doesn mind smears of grease and dirt.
My sista'll reduce yu with sheer muscle hurt.
my sista says no guy goin keep her phone-bound—
with own car mi sista is a wheel-hound.

I sey I wohn get a complex.
I wohn get a complex.
Then I see the muscles my sista flex.

Scribbled Notes Picked up by Owners, and Rewritten
because of bad grammar, bad spelling, bad writing

Letter is signed—YOUR ONE BABY-PERSON.
I know you like me
because you know I like to be tossed up
in the air and caught
and I know you're best
at making laughs.
You know it's great
when you coo and coo on me in smiles
with hugs and tickles and teases.
I rub my legs together.
I do my baby-dance on my back.
My fist hangs on your thumb.
I chuckle. I chuckle, saying
'This face over me is great!'
I say GA, GA, and you know I say
Go-Ahead, Go-Ahead. Make
funny faces talk, sing,
tickle. Please. Make me chuckle
this time, next time,
every time. Now. Please.

Letter from YOUR SPeCiAl-BiG-pUPPy-DOg.
You know I'm so big
I'll soon become a person.
You know I want to know more
of all that you know. Yet
you leave the house, so, so often.
And not one quarrel between us.
Why don't you come home ten times
a day? Come tell me the way
your boss is bad? See me sit,
listening, sad? And you know,
and I know, it's best
when you first come in.

You call my name. And O
I go starry-eyed on you,
can't stop wagging, jumping,
holding, licking your face,
saying, 'D'you know—d'you know—
you're quite, quite a dish!'
Come home—come call my name—
every time thirty minutes pass.

Letter from Your KitTeN-cAT-AlMoSt-BiG-CaT.
You tell me to clear up
the strings of wool off
the floor, just to see how
I slink out the door. But O
you're my mum. Fifty times
big to climb on. You stroke
my back from head to tail.
You tickle my furry throat,
letting my claws needle your side,
and my teeth nibble your hand
till I go quiet. I purr.
I purr like a poor boy
snoring, after gift of a dinner.
I leap into your lap only
to start everything over.

From Your COloURfUl-GUiNeaPig.
You come to me. I shriek
to you, to let you know
I'm a found friend
you can depend on. I know
you long to learn my language.
You talk to me over
and over, in lots
of little words. I listen,
going still, with a quiet heart.
My eyes should go
all in a brighter shine.

Watch my eyes.
Listen my shriek.
You'll hear what I say.

Letter from YOuR RaBbIT.
To you, who belongs to me.
I listen. You know that.
Come see me. Now.
After. Soon. Later. Again.
All Time—talk
with same words you bring
on my face like daybreak
everyday. Stroke me like wind
passing. Then you've come
for heads to be lost together
in a hole in the ground,
in dreams about fields
grown and overgrown.
Watch my ears, you'll see
I catch all you say.
Feel my eyes on you
and you'll hear
'I have space for you
to huddle, in my bed.'

Letter is from YOUR horse.
Though I'm sort of high up and big
I don't boast. I'm not snooty.
I don't get easily cross.
When you come to me, come
with long rope of talk
like I'm a soppy dog.
Stroke me with looks, voice,
hands, together saying,
'Hello big fellow!
Handsome big fellow,
you're a joy on the eye
with broad back under sky.

You're swift like flits
of lightning lifts of feet,
but stand still
to listen to human parrot.'
You talk like that,
I nuzzle you.
Hear when I say,
'Come walk with me,
clop-clopping
with me, side by side.'

You see, I sign a letter myself PIg.
But O most of all
I want you to see
I want us to dig together,
wallow together and share
one bath. I want us to walk
together, all muddy and smart.
I want you to have
my work and my fun.
You give me food, you're gone.
You forget and forget and forget
that if you scratch my back
or rub my belly on and on,
ever so weak I go.
I lie down. I stretch out.
I grunt. I grunt, saying
'Don't. Don't. Don't.
Don't you stop stroking.'

The Donkey and the Man

Duff-Duff rides companion Cranky
up the warm, green and wide hills
daily. But Cranky has a way
of making a donkey statement.

In spite of a waspy whip
stinging hip, and weight
of load sitting on back,
up hill, down hill, on
rocky roads and mud-hole tracks,
Cranky never hurries.

Cranky will just lie down
with the man there on his back,
merely sinks down on tummy
and let Duff-Duff leap from his ride.

Going home, again, today,
Duff-Duff explodes, as usual,
noisy and abusive, dropping
his machete in the road.
He tugs hard at the packed
load, loosening it roughly.

He unfastens one hamper of yams
and the other with cedar shingles
and a young ram. He loosens
firewood and a water pan.

Load unfastened around Cranky,
Duff-Duff pushes, Duff-Duff yells
telling donkey to get up.

But Cranky breathes. Cranky
slackens his girth in relief.
His big eyes go sleepy, as if
to all the man's shouting
and pleading a donkey is deaf.

Then, grunting, Cranky gets up.
Cranky swells himself rigid
like a barrel. Man retightens
its girth, refixes the load
then remounts and tops it all.
Cranky moves off,
relaxing, as best able
to keep his girth slack.

Next day comes. Sunrise begins
to change to the gold of morning.
Cranky sees Duff-Duff.
Donkey trots away
and hides, behind low branches.

Why's your face so full of worry?
Duff-Duff says. You'll see my face
is none too happy either. You know
we climb the hills. And they do.
But nothing makes Cranky hurry.
Man gives him no will.

Cool Time Rhythm Rap

1

You aren't hollow.
Walk and talk big—fellow.
You can't do that
then better can cruise in a yacht.
Still, can't do it?
Then sit—
watch me do it all on TV.

2

Don't stare at my face—
my naked place.

Look. Look at my clothes.
Look. Look at my shoes.

Look. Look at my hair.
Take in all of my all-round flair.

3

Better come out, robber man,
it's up—your robbing plan.
Come out of the bank, d'you hear?
All the police are here.
The lot have you surrounded.
Your high-life hopes are grounded.
Better come out, robber man,
it's up—your robbing plan.

4

Let no certain—person
shake your hand
without your eye fastened
on his other hand.

My Hard Repair Job

In the awful quarrel
we had, my temper burnt
our friendship to cinders.
How can I make it whole again?

This way, that way,
that time, this time,
I pick up the burnt bits,
trying to change them back.

A Toast for Everybody Who Is Growin

A Toast for Everybody Who Is Growin

Somebody who is growin
is a girl or a boy—
I tell yu is a girl or a boy—
with hips gettn broader
than a lickle skirt
and shoulders gettn bigger
than a lickle shirt,
wantin six teachers
through the misery of maths
and one—only one—
who never ever get cross.
O, the coconut—
it come from so far
yu think it would-a get
hello, from a hazelnut.

Somebody who is growin
is a girl or a boy—
I tell yu is a girl or a boy—
who ride a bus to school
like an empty pocket fool
yet really well wantin
own, own-a, BMW
to cruise up West and North
and all aroun SW.
O, the pineapple—
it come from so far
yu think it would-a get
hello, from a apple.

Somebody who is growin
Is a girl or a boy—
I tell yu is a girl or a boy—
who will never get rich
from a no-inflation boom,
will share no Dallas banquet
that come in own sitting-room,
to keep a bodypopper
with a crummy-crummy supper.
O, yu think it would-a mek
a stone scream
rollin down a hill
jumpin in-a stream.
But, in spite of everythin,
everybody who's growin
GO ON, nah! GO ON. Jus do that thing.

Girls Can We Educate We Dads?

Listn the male chauvinist in mi dad—
a girl walkin night street mus be bad.
He dohn sey, the world's a free place
for a girl to keep her unmolested space.
Instead he sey—a girl is a girl.

He sey a girl walkin swingin hips about
call boys to look and shout.
He dohn sey, if a girl have style
she wahn to sey, look
I okay from top to foot.
Instead he sey—a girl is a girl.

Listn the male chauvinist in mi dad—
a girl too laughy-laughy look too glad-glad
jus like a girl too looky-looky roun
will get a pretty satan at her side.
He dohn sey—a girl full of go
dohn wahn stifle talent comin on show.
Instead he sey—a girl is a girl.

A Different Kind of Sunday

You go to church in England,
it isn't the bright Caribbean day,
isn't orange and mango ripening
with fowls raking about under bush.
It's not a donkey and mule holy day
after they'd bathed in sea in sunrise,
not the same dream of Jesus
when you are melting,
though you fan yourself and everybody else.

You go to church in England,
it's no banana and coconut trees
making a little breeze look merry
in middleday sunhot
when goats pant in mottled shades.

You go to church in England,
cleaned-up people listen to parson
but trucks aren't parked in palmtree yards
when loose boys fix bicycles,
birdsong stripes the day like ribbons,
the sea has a sabbath day seasound.

You go to church in England,
parson is same preacher-Paul strong-man
beating the air to beat up badness
but John-crows don't glide around blue sky
to be looked at out of window.
And good things at the end aren't
like best lemonade, iced up,
and dinner added-to all week
to go with family jokes kept Sunday-quiet
before the walking-out in evening shadows.

You go to church in England,
you sit in a groan
of traffic on and on around you,
where, O, the sun is so so forgetful.

Banana and Mackerel

O look ow markit full—
ow markit of London pull
field crop them come a-follah we
across Caribbean sea.

Look pon white and yellow yam,
pon ripe plantain and green Lacatan.
Look pon big, deep-flesh avocadoes,
ackee and red sweet potatoes.

Lord, people-food come a Englan
and stop Westindian food ration.
Back-home flavours deh yah
like all fish, fowl and fruit colour.

Yu can get yu spices and sorrel,
can av bwoil banana and mackerel.
O fishin and cuttin and pickin follah we
across Caribbean sea.

Lacatan—a variety of bananas
deh yah—are here

Breath Pon Wind

Mi mum is funny, funny, yu know.
Listn to mi mum to mi big brodda, na—

    'Boy! Have yuself lost in-a youth gang,
    yu only can see notn wrang.

    Yu cahn see, cos yu eyes
    no longa yu own eyes,
    cos they well-well seized in-a gang control
    to get all a yu, spoilers, feelin bold,
    to get all yu good sense gone too scarce
    and it easy to throw brick pon glass place
    and yu know notn ow yu come lan
    straight in-a police van.

    Boy! Yu mus learn to turn man, yes,
    but noh by gettn in-a fool-fool mess.
    A boy dohn have to go all boasify—
    bloated, to mek him look smart guy—
    so it easy to toss foot up pon train seat
    and smoke cigarette like a stupid sweet.

    Boy! Yu goin answer me?
    Yu goin answer me?
    Yu a-hear what I a-sey
    or all is waste breath wind blow away?'

Wahn hear mi mum to mi big brodda, na!
Mi mum is funny, funny, yu know.

boasify—to be conceited and boastful

Mum Dad and Me

My parents grew among palmtrees,
in sunshine strong and clear.
I grow in weather that's pale,
misty, watery or plain cold,
around back streets of London.

Dad swam in warm sea, at my age.
I swim in a roofed pool.
Mum—she still doesn't swim.

Mum went to an open village market
at my age. I go to a covered
arcade one with her now.
Dad works most Saturdays.

At my age Dad played
cricket with friends.
Mum helped her mum, or talked
shouting halfway up a hill.
Now I read or talk on the phone.

With her friends Mum's mum washed
clothes on a river-stone. Now
washing-machine washes our clothes.
We save time to eat to TV,
never speaking.

My dad longed for a freedom in Jamaica.
I want a greater freedom.
Mum prays for us, always.

Mum goes to church
some evenings and Sundays.
I go to the library.
Dad goes for his darts at the local.

Mum walked everywhere, at my age.
Dad rode a donkey.
Now I take a bus
or catch the underground train.

Black Kid in a New Place

I'm here, I see
I make a part of a little planet
here, with some of everybody now.

I stretch myself, I see
I'm like a migrant bird
who will not return from here.

I shake out colourful wings.
I set up a palmtree bluesky
here, where winter mists were.

Using what time tucked in me, I see
my body pops with dance.
Streets break out in carnival.

Rooms echo my voice. I see
I was not a migrant bird. I am
a transplanted sapling, here, blossoming.

Let Me Rap You My Orbital Map

At a disco girls cluster and dance me in,
at a party everyone knows I don't take gin.
I walk in a room that's tangled with fight
I cool it, calm it, make things right—
shove a head back on where it came adrift;
shove an arm back on where it had left.
Kisses wash me for that ease in my tough;
gifts are piled on me though already I've enough.
    Cos—I'm a social rover,
    I overspend—I'm a goldcard lover,
    but man, you know, rhythm's the thing
    and girl, you know, I got the style that sings.

I fix it at cricket I'm top run-getter,
fix it at football I'm that wall-goalkeeper.
My chest is first on the tape when I run;
I box ten rounds—it's ten k.o's of fun.
Yet who can say I do not care—
for a change, I pamper, I fix my hair.
I meet the town, I expose what's vile;
I meet my crowd I'm all a smile.
    Cos—I'm a social rover,
    I overspend—I'm a goldcard lover,
    but man, you know, rhythm's the thing
    and girl, you know, I got the style that sings.

So warm, my handshake sets people on fire.
Such a storm—ceilings come down when I holler.
I don't stand by and cry I won't be a spy;
I don't tell a private or a worldwide lie.
Clothes fashion wise
I'm same me—no disguise
relaxin, creatin, plush in my red Porsche
cruisin, or just dashin by—woosh!
    Cos—I'm a social rover,
    I overspend—I'm a goldcard lover,
    but man, you know, rhythm's the thing
    and girl, you know, I got the style that sings.

See, I'm me—one who shuns no test;
one of the few who finds the zest
makin music in my talk
doin a dance in my walk.
And people gasp when I take the stage—
struck with my songs, their sweetness, their rage,
sharin my hop from star to star
as I slam on my silver guitar.
    Cos—I'm a social rover,
    I overspend—I'm a goldcard lover,
    but man, you know, rhythm's the thing
    and girl, you know, I got the style that sings.

What We Said
Sitting Making Fantasies

What We Said Sitting Making Fantasies

1

I want a talking dog wearing a cap
who can put on gloves
and go to my mum when I'm playing
and she wants a job done.

2

I'd like a great satellite-looking dish
in my garden, drawing together all sounds
of birds' voices, cats' mewing and fighting
crickets' chirping, dogs' barking and fighting
frogs' croaking, guineapigs' squeaking
bicycle-bells ringing, babies' crying
trains' passing, firecrackers' bursts and bangs
into one loud orchestral work
playing once every hour day and night
a new composition every time
so an audience overbrims my garden.

3

At last I have my anger breathalyser
that shows them all—
parents, teachers, friends—
the fires they start
when they make me cross.
I just whip out
my Angerlyser.
Offender watches me blow
hard into it
and sees it swell
its fierce balloon of green
then black then red
and sees it drop and burst
into a flame, three colours
of horned heads and teeth

flaring, jumping, hissing
popping, spluttering—
all round the culprit's feet.
And I just walk away.

4

I'd like a white bull with one horn only
and it's black, and one eyepatch that's black,
and one stripe of red like a bright sash
all around his throat, side and back.
And my bull windowshops from shop to shop
on High Street on his own. And when
my bull moves, his whole red sash flashes
buttons of white lights
advertising my mum's curtain and wallpaper
shop, saying, PICTURES NOT CURTAINS. PETALS
NOT PAPER. FLORAL HOUSE FOR FASHION.

5

My first solo trial flight, you see.
I'm in my flying craft I made myself,
strapped in my seat. Gyrocompass, like
every clockface instrument,
every switch, button and lever, is handy.
In constructing my craft I considered
all problems that affect flying stability.
I considered the aircraft's 'angles of attack'.
I considered its 'lift–drag ratio'.
I considered its 'total reaction'.
Yet when I operate the craft to go
forward, it zooms upward, climbing.
I operate it to descend, it levels
itself, it shoots away forward.
I operate it to climb, my craft spins
round and round and dives
to a perfect touchdown
and settles itself, purring like a cat.
I press a button, I'm unstrapped.
I press a button, I'm flicked up

and out, ejected on to my feet, in front
of the Queen, with her dogs in her garden.
'Hello,' she says. 'You must be Robin Flyer!'
'Yes, mam,' I say. She walks forward.
'Last week, your great-granma was a hundred.'
'Yes, mam. Your telegram came. We celebrated.'
'In her letter of thanks, your gran said
not to be surprised if you dropped
in. And here you are! Well—
stay for tea. Won't you? All
my grandchildren are coming.'
Naturally, I stay for tea, with dogs
and everybody there in the garden.

6

I'd like to have a purple pigeon
who flies up to heaven
and comes back rose-red
flying with trails of pale rainbow ribbons
straight through my window
into my bedroom.

7

I have a three-legged donkey.
I have my three-legged donkey just to see
how he dips his head when he walks
and quickens it up when he gallops.

8

I'd like to see cats with stubby wings
who just before their wings get raised
for a leap on to a bird, they set off
the loudest high pitched siren sound
from the cat's mouth. O, it's a scream
something earsplitting terrible.
Often you see cats losing distance
flying in desperation behind birds
and their on-and-on wailing
scream goes on, cracking up the air.

Shapes and Actions

Like roundness of the rotating globe
head and wheel and ball make me think and sigh

Like gliding swim of a small or giant fish
drifting moon makes me think and sigh

Like a tramp's hunt in a waiting dustbin
a fox's city-search for food makes me think and sigh

Like a sloth's slow-motion climb
creeping-in sea-tide makes me think and sigh

Like humans and animals everywhere asleep
inner work of winter trees makes me think and sigh

Like unknown red wings taking off in flight
flame-leaps in open space make me think and sigh

A Story about Afiya

Afiya has fine black skin
that shows off her white clothes
and big brown eyes that laugh
and long limbs that play.
She has a white summer frock
she wears and washes every night
that every day picks on something
to collect, strangely.

Afiya passes sunflowers and finds
the yellow fringed black faces there,
imprinted on her frock, all over.
Another time she passes red roses
and there the clustered bunches
are, imprinted on her frock.

She walks through high grass and sees
butterflies and all kinds
of slender stalks and petals
patterned on her back and front
and are still there, after
she has washed her dress.

Afiya stands. She watches
the sharp pictures in colour,
untouched by her wash.
Yet, next morning, every day,
the dress is cleared and ready,
hanging white as new paper.

Then pigeons fly up before her
and decorate her dress
with their flight and group design.
Afiya goes to the zoo;
she comes back with two tigers
together, on her back and on her front.

She goes to the seaside;
she comes home with fishes
under ruffled waves
in the whole stretch of sea
imprinted on her dress.

She walks between round and towered
boulders and takes them away,
pictured on her.

Always Afiya is amazed,
just like when she comes home
and finds herself covered
with windswept leaves
of October, falling.

Afiya—a Swahili name, meaning health, is pronounced Ah-fee-yah

Spite Shots Labels

Wouldn't it be good
if as they grow
bodies could show
rammed-in pins and nails exposed—
spite bullets, all tagged—
at head, hand, tummy, bum,
showing where they came from,
why launched
and when due to be returned.

Body-steadier

Body-steadier

Falling-off has a wobble-trouble
that tips you off your bike.
But let body-steadier handle it,
like talking and skipping same time,
you see how you break
that can't-ride strike, and fly
away on your bicycle.
You see you just jump on—
spin wheels
round garden path
round playing-field
round streets ruled by friends,
by show-offs, meanies, bullies.

Whistling will curl up
and hide itself in you.
But get breath to grab it—
no sweat. No trouble.
You see that you have
exact flutey spout of a mouth
uncoiling a whistling, like ribbons.
You stand, you watch
the great dog-run of Raff
in swift speed to you
for a lark, all around the park.

Swimming knows a sinking dodge
that ties bricks on arms and legs.
But beat it, get the knack—
feel bricks cut loose, and go.
You feel all-action limbs
doing the swimming trick.
You just splash in—
become a busy dolphin. Become
a big brilliant frog. You float
like a seagull or a log.
You swim in a pool like a crazy water fool.

Leaps of Feeling

There's nothing like a party. Nothing.
  Last night
another dream. The swinging roomful
of zodiac signs.
Showplace of trends and flair.
A piece of spectacle—everybody.
Steps unknown rush in and dance you.

  Nothing like a party.
Food isn't for table.
Music's a crowd's own age.
Joy of a drink is the slow sweaty sip.
Wit is how it shoots down brilliance.
Malice of a gossip is how
it is spiced up.

  Nothing like a party.
A known voice shatters you.
A known hug collects you up.
A new squeeze charges like champagne.
All dream girls. All show blokes.
Dazzlers rave up those who
only manage a glimmer.
To be, you become
a room of pleasure-pulsing.

  Nothing like a party. Nothing.
Reality isn't big enough.
Wishes die.
But hopes mount like flames.
Mixes push somebody
here and there over the top.
  It's a night of clusters:
it works leaps of feeling.
Just can't find where else
I'm more discovered.

Disco Date, 1980

In rainbow beams high and low,
lights move—on the go.

Place is full—full already.
Session's right on—steady.
Singer is rock-style.
Girls fancy they top all styles.

Anything goes
yet flash crews make separate shows.

Sounds lash, sounds bite,
people writhe.

Dreads flash locks.
Chains flash Punks.
Fresh green girls dance in groups.
Trendies too dance in groups.
Posers pose at doing the best.
Loners refrain from situations of test.

Not here to stand and stare,
though alone, I'll get in there.

In heavy sounds I show torment
like all, in best garments,
next to those who do the 'break',
next to clowns and freaks,
while Posers pretend
and Trendies take sips according to trend.

I rest. I watch body antics
with all the gymnastics—
the hundred-yards on one spot,
the marathons on one spot,
the Punks, the Dreads,
New Romantics and Skinheads,
the Clones, the Straights—
all in a jump-up as if they really are mates.

When I Dance

When I dance it isn't merely
That music absorbs my shyness,
My laughter settles in my eyes,
My swings of arms convert my frills
As timing tunes my feet with floor
As if I never just looked on.

It is that when I dance
O music expands my hearing
And it wants no mathematics,
It wants no thinking, no speaking,
It only wants all my feeling
In with animation of place.

When I dance it isn't merely
That surprises dictate movements,
Other rhythms move my rhythms,
I uncradle rocking-memory
And skipping, hopping and running
All mix movements I balance in.

It is that when I dance
I'm costumed in a rainbow mood,
I'm okay at any angle,
Outfit of drums crowds madness round,
Talking winds and plucked strings conspire,
Beat after beat warms me like sun.

When I dance it isn't merely
I shift bodyweight balances
As movement amasses my show,
I celebrate each dancer here,
No sleep invades me now at all
And I see how I am tireless.

It is that when I dance
I gather up all my senses
Well into hearing and feeling,
With body's flexible postures
Telling their poetry in movement
And I celebrate all rhythms.

Boxer Man in-a Skippin Workout

Skip on big man, steady steady.
Giant, skip-dance easy easy!
Broad and tall a-work shaped limbs,
a-move sleek self with style well trimmed.
Gi rhythm your ease in bein strong.
Movement is a meanin and a song.
    Tek your little trips in your skips, man.
    Be that dancer-runner man.

You so easy easy. Go-on na big man!
Fighter man is a rhythm man
full of go fine and free.
Movement is a dream and a spree.
You slow down, you go fast.
Sweat come oil your body like race horse.
    Tek your little trips in your skips, man.
    Be that dancer-runner man—big man!

Quick Ball Man

for Michael Holding

Bowlerman bowlerman—
O such a wheel-action is quick ball man!

A warrior man
thas such an all-right movement man.

All day him run races,
a-run those poundin riddim paces.

And wicket them a-fly like bullet hit them.
Ball a-hit batsman leg cos it a-fool him.

Batsman a-get caught.
More a-get out fo nought.

More a-come pad-up with runs in them head
but them jus a-come to walk back dead.

And bowlerman is noh jus bowlerman.
The man turn heself now in-a batsman.

And him noh wahn one-one run to get match fix.
Him only wahn six back-a six.

Soh him noh loveless.
Hug-up is regula fram all the mates.

Bowlerman bowlerman—
O such a wheel-action is quick ball man.

Don't Howl

In play we play
it's stretch we stretch.
Not war we war.
    And I tag along with it.

Get shin clobbered, don't howl.
Get fouled and hurt, don't shout.
Get knee cut, don't bleed.
Get knocked down, don't die.
Stretching game it is.
Not war.
    And I tag along with it.

It's the grunt in our hit-out
they want in our muscles.
Pull of the pack in the race flat out.
Kick in the ball that makes it a goal.
Reach in the arm that nets the ball.
    And I tag along with it.

Run. Jump. Swing. Pull.
Strain!
It's stretch you stretch.
Not war you war.

Whip-up yourself beyond yourself.
Keep pressing till you drop.
It's stretch we stretch.
Win or lose, they tell us,
it's the stretch we want.
    And I tag along with it.

Pair of Hands Against Football

Opposition
Supporters: You make the cash-tills ring.
You make crowds of people sing.

Goalkeeper's
Supporters: You make feet jump into a tackle
then make them move into a dribble.
Football—you draw a million eyes.
Football—we love your ruses.
You lead quick feet to strike
and others to attack the strike
to outsmart TWO HANDS—
our GOALKEEPER'S HANDS.

Goalkeeper: Well, artful ball from the grass.
you shall not pass
HANDS like wall
for you football,
stopping your triumph-roar
'cos I'm goalkeeper, you hear—
HANDS OF TWO
against eleven heads and feet of twenty-two

Opposition
Supporters: You make the crowd moan.
You make the crowd go mean.
You make the crowd leap up aggrieved.
You make the crowd sit down relieved.

Goalkeeper's
Supporters: Come on zigzagging like a snake.
You find you have no gate!
Come on flying like a bird.
See—no cage for a bird!
Come straight like a bullet.
See—you're in HANDS like a wallet!

Goalkeeper: Well, artful ball from the grass,
you shall not pass
HANDS like wall
for you football,

stopping your triumph-roar
'cos I'm goalkeeper, you hear—
HANDS OF TWO
against eleven heads and feet of twenty-two

Opposition
Supporters:

You make the crowd feel relaxed.
You make the crowd feel whacked.

Goalkeeper's
Supporters:

You make a foot land you on a thigh,
make another drive you sky high,
make others turn you into a hare;
you come—our HANDS are there.
You bring a group, close, busy, like lions.
You get knocked up into HANDS of iron.

Goalkeeper:

Well, artful ball from the grass,
you shall not pass
HANDS like wall
for you football,
stopping your triumph-roar
'cos I'm goalkeeper, you hear—
HANDS OF TWO
against eleven heads and feet of twenty-two.

Goalkeeper's
Supporters:

You make us feel washed up
but roar at raised winner's cup.

Goalkeeper:

Well, artful ball from the grass,
you shall not pass
HANDS like wall
for you football,
stopping your triumph-roar
'cos I'm goalkeeper, you hear—
HANDS OF TWO
against eleven heads and feet of twenty-two.

The Barkday Party

For my dog's birthday party
I dressed like a bear.
My friends came as lions
and tigers and wolves and monkeys.
At first, Runabout couldn't believe
the bear was really me. But
he became his old self again
when I fitted on his magician's top hat.
Runabout became the star, running about
jumping up on chairs and tables
barking at every question asked him.
Then, in their ordinary clothes,
my friend Brian and his dad arrived
with their boxer, Skip. And with us
knowing nothing about it, Brian's dad
mixed the dog's party meat and milk
with wine he brought.We started
singing. Runabout started to yelp.
All the other six dogs joined—
yelping
    Happy Barkday to you
     Happy Barkday to you
    Happy Barkday Runabout
    Happy Barkday to you!

One

One

Only one of me
and nobody can get a second one
from a photocopy machine.

Nobody has the fingerprints I have.
Nobody can cry my tears, or laugh my laugh
or have my expectancy when I wait.

But anybody can mimic my dance with my dog.
Anybody can howl how I sing out of tune.
And mirrors can show me multiplied
many times, say, dressed up in red
or dressed up in grey.

Nobody can get into my clothes for me
or feel my fall for me, or do my running.
Nobody hears my music for me, either.

I am just this one.
Nobody else makes the words
I shape with sound, when I talk.

But anybody can act how I stutter in a rage.
Anybody can copy echoes I make.
And mirrors can show me multiplied
many times, say, dressed up in green
or dressed up in blue.

Boy Alone at Noon

Completely central over me
is this lace of sun
topping trees

The world is white
and green and shadowy
I am almost enclosed from sky

The river lolls lapping
over rough tongued rocks
and leaf rottings

A dragonfly takes two dips
it flops in again
it goes with a flip

The nutmeg trees
have pods popped with nuts
I smell hot grass

I smell tree blossoms
I wish I could know
a lot of reasons

Busy birds go stateless
I have no government either
My father is strong and pocketless

The track waits to my hut
I better fill my bamboo with water
and go on up

Kept Home

I look out of my high up window.
I see chimney tops, fences, scattered trees,
in this sunny summer-Saturday.

Our white cat strolls
across the neighbour's newly cut grass.
Birds are noisy.
A wind teases branches
and gardens of flowers.

I can't see far on my left.
The silver birch spreads
elegant branches before me,
fluttering its leaves like
a lady's shiny frills in sunlight.

Girls and boys play football,
smaller ones are swinging,
in the playground
and view of the church...

Out and out, past all streets
and housetops and trees, the sky
touches our Lookfar Hill,
with a smoky white light surrounding.

When holidays come, any day now,
and I'm well, fit again,
I shall clamber up
Lookfar's hillside tracks...

An iron bird roars...
Aeroplane breaks the clouds.
It sails in open space.
Who are on board?
Who? I wonder...

Travelling or staying at home,
people wait to get somewhere—
wait for something to happen,
something to end, begin or develop...

Sunlight floods my room suddenly.
Shadows move on one wall
like reflections
of a busy open flame.

Sounds of motor cars get louder.
Every day our world is its own
moving-picture show...
What new character can I add?...

Coming Home On My Own

I slept with fourteen strange
people, in the youth-hostel room.
All of us had to get up early.
I turned and opened my eyes—
it was bright open daylight.
Right away, everybody turned over
too, woke up, began to talk.
And it was good how we washed,
dressed and made breakfast together.
But we broke up. We separated
on foot, on bicycles
and I by bus—waving goodbye.

Different Feelings

Lying in bed, hearing
silence of snowfall.

Eating, full of the expected.
Now lost, empty, exhausted.

Running in the open
sweating, after a ball.

Getting Nowhere

Next week I'll leave school.
Next week, nil, fulltime—
me—for good!

Yonks now
nobody bothered.
No teacher scrawled, 'work harder'.
Or, 'Use your potential'.

They'd twigged on.
Their words were whispers
to a rock. So
They gave up on me.

They had no grasp—
none to give.
Had no power to kick
my motor into clatter.

Not to lift a bat, next week
I'm bowled out for duck.
Year in year out
terrible need took
nothing teachers served.

I couldn't win them.
They couldn't win me.
Their mouthings reached me jammed.
So routines to me will end next week.

Lamp of workshop drawing got built
only as far as the base
and abandoned. Made scrap.

And a relief will grab them.
Relieved, the teachers will sigh—
'Clearly, a non-achiever.'

Next week, I'll leave school
but stay held on poverty street.
Held hostage by myself, they'll say.

Take Away Some but Leave Some

Take the nastiness that turns me into disgrace;
leave me words that make me a sun-face.

Take the absence that turns me skeleton;
leave me that feast of farmer and son.

Take the silence that's unrisen cake at my meal;
leave me roundness of rolling ball and wheel.

Take my old clothes for new in latest trends;
leave me all my old friends.

Skateboard Flyer

Please Mum please
not again back-to-school
for I-man-skater.
I must rush it, Mum, rush it
and lift up high
over ransacked dustbins
over streets of rubbish
over every tower block
and be highrise—I, up and over.
Mum—enough times you say
you want me off the streets.

Please Mum please
not again back-to-school
for free skateboard Rasta.
I must rush it and lift
over bashed-in street lamps
to drop down on moving roller coaster
and lift off over chimney tops
over mashed up playgrounds—
gliding over, just gliding and gliding.
Mum—enough times you say
you want me off the streets.

Please Mum please
not again back-to-school
for I-man-skater
who must rush it
and shoot from star to star
and be gone
over police stations with arrested people
and be gone
over every schooling barrier
and be gone
over the terror of faces.
Please—not school again.
Mum—enough times you say
you want me off the streets.

Barriers

Barriers

How can he wrench away
steely handgrips
that captured his body
not so much for flesh caught wild
as for energy made gold?

How can he lift out
his layers of doctrine
about 'GREAT MEN'—
who headed mass killings
that left him to walk with wounds and hurts?

How can he remove
smooth stony voices
piled around his head
not so much to entomb him dead
as entomb him breathing?

How can he simply stop
ever oncoming feet
in rooms, alleyways, in the street
trampling him, trampling him,
to go back, stay in—stay inward?

It Seems I Test People

My skin sun-mixed like basic earth
my voice having tones of thunder
my laughter working all of me as I laugh
my walk motioning strong swings
it seems I test people

Always awaiting a move
waiting always to recreate my view
my eyes packed with hellos behind them
my arrival bringing departures
it seems I test people

Dreaming Black Boy

I wish my teacher's eyes wouldn't
go past me today. Wish he'd know
it's okay to hug me when I kick
a goal. Wish I myself wouldn't
hold back when an answer comes.
I'm no woodchopper now
like all ancestors.

I wish I could be educated
to the best of tune up, and earn
good money and not sink to lick
boots. I wish I could go on every
crisscross way of the globe
and no persons or powers or
hotel keepers would make it a waste.

I wish life wouldn't spend me out
opposing. Wish same way creation
would have me stand it would have
me stretch, and hold high, my voice
Paul Robeson's, my inside eye
a sun. Nobody wants to say
hello to nasty answers.

I wish torch throwers of night
would burn lights for decent times.
Wish plotters in pyjamas would pray
for themselves. Wish people wouldn't
talk as if I dropped from Mars.

I wish only boys were scared
behind bravados, for I could suffer.
I could suffer a big big lot.
I wish nobody would want to earn
the terrible burden I can suffer.

What Do We Do with a Variation?

What do we do with a difference?
Do we stand and discuss its oddity
or do we ignore it?

Do we shut our eyes to it
or poke it with a stick?
Do we clobber it to death?

Do we move around it in rage
and enlist the rage of others?
Do we will it to go away?

Do we look at it in awe
or purely in wonderment?
Do we work for it to disappear?

Do we pass it stealthily
or change route away from it?
Do we will it to become like ourselves?

What do we do with a difference?
Do we communicate to it,
let application acknowledge it
for barriers to fall down?

City Nomad

Indifferent to crowds
indifferent to weather
he goes about arrested.

Schooled on chasms unbridgeable
he uses pain of traps
to communicate.

Own jury own court
he waves and gestures
at his own cross-questioning.

Drifting this morning
he arrives and gazes
at the city's river.

It becomes a shore like a dream
where he is lost
and the sea lashes monstrous rocks.

And he's confused
with suggestions of travel—
going and coming and being.

Arms open, legs apart—
a stare and a grin on his face—
he roars and beckons.

He embraces a towering wave, falls
in a shawl of mist and tightens shut eyes
to keep out faces looking down on him.

Drifting again this evening
he searches
for another bed.

One shadowy thought
stays and absorbs
his entire volition—

somehow
somewhere
someone must have wronged him.

Sunny Market Song

Sunny Market Song

1st Voice: Coffee
                     Spiced chocolate
                     Ackee

                     White yam
                     Yellow Yam
                     Juicy melon

                     Breadfruit
                     Grapefruit
                     Arrowroot

2nd Voice: I want some cinnamon and tamarind, mam

3rd Voice: Buy quatty wo't' noh, gal—
                     Buy quatty wo't'
                                       (FOWLS CACKLE)

1st Voice: Tapioca
                     Sarsaparilla
                     Cassava

                     Snapper fish
                     Fresh fish
                     Strong charcoal

                     Dry coconuts
                     Water coconuts
                     Mango

2nd Voice: I want some cloves and lemon, mam

3rd Voice: Buy quatty wo't' noh, gal—
                     Buy quatty wo't'
                                       (A PIG SQUEALS)

1st Voice: Custard apple
               Ripe pineapple
               Sweet potatoes

               Cho-cho
               Callalu
               Coco

               Soursop
               Sweetsop
               Sorrel

2nd Voice: I want some nutmeg and ginger, mam

3rd Voice: Buy quatty wo't' noh, gal—
               Buy quatty wo't'

                                            (A GOAT BLEATS)

1st Voice: Foo-foo plantain
               Ripe plantain
               Papaw

               Fever grass
               Strong-back herb
               Mount'n honey comb

               Orange
               Cabbage
               Hominy corn

2nd Voice: I want some allspice and pepper, mam

3rd Voice: Buy quatty wo't' noh, gal—
               Buy quatty wo't'

                                            (DOGS BARK)

1st Voice:	Fresh whelks
	Beeswax
	Floor dye
	Blackeye peas
	Congo peas
	Okra
	Jackass rope
	Raw sugar
	Ripe bananas
2nd Voice:	I want some scallion and annatto, mam
3rd Voice:	Buy quatty wo't' noh, gal—
	Buy quatty wo't'

(A DONKEY BRAYS)

For individual or group performance:
1st Voice represents general market voices.
2nd Voice, girl buying spices and seasoning from
3rd Voice, stallholder, who could be voiced by audience.
Quatty is Jamaican word for penny-half-penny.
Jackass rope is slang term used for leaves of locally grown tobacco twisted
into form of long rope, coiled for handling.

Diggin Sing

Whai-O! Man, go-on O.
Push with cowskin boot.
Go man, go-on O.
Work you hand, work foot.
Go man, go-on O.
Turn ground with strong man.
Go man, go-on O.
Turn Mas Tom Big Land.
Go man, go-on O.
Woman see you strong.
Go man, go-on O.
Jackass hear your song.
Go man, go-on O.
A friendly work, noh!
A friendly work O.

Whai-O! Man, go-on O.
Want like stone want ground.
Go man, go-on O.
Push hard down to groan.
Go man, go-on O.
Know ground like seeker.
Go man, go-on O.
Know ground a giver.
Go man, go-on O.
Children see you good.
Go man, go-on O.
Dog see you it god.
Go man, go-on O.
A friendly work, noh!
A friendly work O.
Go man, go-on O.
A friendly work, noh!
A friendly work O ...

Friday Work

Man, yu should av come
up mountain lan on Friday.
Puppa dig groun and pile up
stones. We boys clear up and pile
stones too. Wild bees move
in-a swarm over trees.

Yu should av come, man.
Branches fan sunlight or jus
stay thick, with gold bed of leaves
with scorpions, centipedes—
conies under, in their hole.
Johnchewhits sing their name
repeatin like dunce-head.
Woodpeckers knock, and fight-and-fly
and scream with laugh.

Man, yu should av come.
Hill them marked up with bird hollerin
man choppin, jackass brayin
we fill we goady
down at the gully stream.
And jus as Mumma fix we up
with roast yam lunch, a mongoose
up straight on back legs
did spy on we. But
we drink coconut water.
We eat mango.
O, yu should av come, man.

Johnchewhit—a smallish white-bellied visiting bird to Jamaica: as it searches
for food it tirelessly sings the sound that it is named after.
goady—a calabash goard for keeping water to drink.

Me go a Granny Yard

Wha mek yu go Granny Yard?
Me go Granny Yard
fi go get sorrel drink.
An dat a really really true?
Cahn yu hear a true?
Yu noh did go fi notn else?
Dohn yu hear a notn else?

Wha mek yu go Granny Yard?
Me go Granny Yard
fi go get bwoil puddn.
An dat a really really true?
Cahn yu hear a true?
Yu noh did go fi notn else?
Dohn yu hear a notn else?

Wha mek yu go Granny Yard?
Me go Granny Yard
fi go get orange wine.
An dat a really really true?
Cahn yu hear a true?
Yu noh did go fi notn else?
Dohn yu hear a notn else?

Wha mek yu go Granny Yard?
Me go Granny Yard
fi go get cokenat cake.
An dat a really really true?
Cahn yu hear a true?
Yu noh did go fi notn else?
Dohn yu hear a notn else?

Wha mek yu go Granny Yard?
Me go Granny Yard
fi go get lemonade.
An dat a really really true?
Cahn yu hear a true?
Yu noh did go fi notn else?
Dohn yu hear a notn else?

Wha mek yu go Granny Yard?
    Me go Granny Yard
    fi go get ginger cookies.
An dat a really really true?
    Cahn yu hear a true?
Yu noh did go fi notn else?
    Dohn yu hear a notn else?

Wha mek yu go Granny Yard?
    Me go Granny Yard
    fi go hide from punishment.
Fi go hide from punishment?
    Fi go hide from punishment!

Riddle Poems

1

        Riddle my this, riddle my that—
        guess my riddle or perhaps not.
What is it you pass going to town
that faces you, and coming from town it
faces you and hasn't moved?

        —A tree.

2

        Riddle my this, riddle my that—
        guess my riddle or perhaps not.
Boy is sent for something;
something comes back before boy—why?

        —Boy climbs tree, picks
        coconut and drops it.

3

        Riddle my this, riddle my that—
        guess my riddle or perhaps not.
Little pools
cluster in my father's yard,
a speck in one and it overflows—
what is it?

        —Somebody's eye
        with dust in it.

4

        Riddle my this, riddle my that—
        guess my riddle or perhaps not.
What's hearty as a heart, round as a ring,
dayworker, nightworker, and never eats?

        —A pocket watch.

5

Riddle my this, riddle my that—
guess my riddle or perhaps not.
What follows king walking, yet stays
watching beggar curled up?

—The moon
big and bright.

6

Riddle my this, riddle my that—
guess my riddle or perhaps not.
Rooms are full, hall is full, but
you can't use a spoonful—
what is it?

—Flames and smoke
of a house on fire.

7

Riddle my this, riddle my that—
guess my riddle or perhaps not.
Eyes ablaze looking up,
Four-Legs crouch near Four-Legs—
what is it?

—Dog by dinner table
begging.

8

Riddle my this, riddle my that—
guess my riddle or perhaps not.
Waltzing for leaves
waltzing on grass
and put back to stand in corner—
what is it?

—Garden broom that sweeps
and is put away.

9

        Riddle my this, riddle my that—
        guess my riddle or perhaps not.
Little Miss Singer brushes her dress,
piece falls out that can only grow back—
what is it?

        —Dropped feather
        while bird preens.

10

        Riddle my this, riddle my that—
        guess my riddle or perhaps not.
What is vessel of gold sent off
to hold flesh and blood?

        —Gift of a ring.

11

        Riddle my this, riddle my that—
        guess my riddle or perhaps not.
Hill is my pillow, I have my own bed,
I stretch out, then I roll
side to side—
what am I?

        —A river from its source
        to meeting
        and mixing with the sea.

Song of the Sea and People

Shell of the conch was sounded,
sounded like foghorn.
Women rushed to doorways,
to fences, to gatateways, and watched.
Canoe made from cotton tree
came sailing shoulder high, from up
mountain-pass down to the sea.
  They stared
   at many men under canoe.
  The mothers and children stared.

Shell of the conch was sounded,
sounded like foghorn.
Women rushed to seaside.
Canoes had come in,
come in from way out
of big sea, loaded
with fish, crabs and lobsters.
  They stared
   at sea-catch.
  The mothers and children stared.

Shell of the conch was sounded,
sounded like foghorn.
Women rushed to seaside.
Canoe out of cotton tree had thrown men,
thrown them into deep sea.
Deep sea swallowed men.
Big sea got boat back.
  They stared
   at empty canoe.
  The mothers and children stared.

Nativity Play Plan

Church Leader: Sistas and broddas and everybody,
same like we did sey—
we a-go keepup Jesus birtday.

Members: Yes! Yes!
We a-go keepup Jesus birtday.

Church Leader: Mista Daaswell, bring yu donkey
Mas Pinnty yu bring yu pony.
All will behave good-good with clappin and praisin.

Mista Slim, yu bring two sheep
wha will neither move nor sleep.
Faada B—two bright wing fowl
wha will look like them nevva bawl.

Sistas and broddas and everybody,
we a-go keepup Jesus birthday.
We sey we a-go do that.
A wha we sey we a-go do?

Members: We a-go keepup Jesus birtday.
Yes! Yes!
We a-go keepup Jesus birtday.

Church Leader:	Cousin Sue, bring yu big sow. Aunt Cita, bring yu red cow. All will behave good-good with singin and dancin.
	Beagle and Man-Tom and Big Ben, yu come turn in-a Wise Men. Modda M will bring her new-new child to be the new Jesus child.
	Sistas and broddas and everybody, we a-go keepup Jesus birtday. We sey we a-go do that. A wha we sey we a-go do?
Members:	We a-go keepup Jesus birtday. Yes! Yes! We a-go keepup Jesus birtday...

Jamaican Caribbean Proverbs

(On marriage)
Befoh yu marry keep two yeye opn, afta yu marry shet one.
(Before marriage keep two eyes open, after marriage shut one.)

(On the attraction to something sweet)
Maskita oftn go a village fi syrup but noh always get e.
(The mosquito often goes to the village for syrup but doesn't always get it.)

(On the way the human condition is similar)
Ebery fambly av e bruk foot.
(Every family has its deformity [or its inflicted cruelty].)

Yu neber si kickin-cow widout kickin-calf.
(You never see a cow that kicks who doesn't produce a calf that kicks.)

(On how you can be different from the way you look)
Plenty a mauger cow yu si a common, a bull mumma.
(Many an underfed cow in the pasture is mother of a bull.)

(On using someone else's trouble to profit by)
When yu si yu neighbour beard ketch a-fire, tek water wet fi yu.
(When you see your neighbour's beard on fire, take some water and wet your own.)

(On vanity)
Peacock hide him foot when him hear bout him tail.
(The peacock hides its leg when its tail gets praises.)

If nightingale sing too sweet, jealousy wi kill him mumma.
(If the nightingale sings too sweetly, jealousy will kill its mother.)

Boastin man brodda a de liard.
(The boaster will make out someone else is the liar.)

De great fool him proud like a dog wid two-tail.
(The great fool is as proud as a dog with two tails.)

De man all honey, fly dem gwine nyam him up.
(The man who is all honey, flies are going to eat him up.)

(On the need to first protect yourself if you are going to be insulting or abusive)
Noh cuss alligator 'long-mout' till yu cross riber.
(Don't call an alligator a 'long-mouth' till you have crossed the river.)

Lickle axe cut down big tree!
(A little axe can cut down a big tree.)

(On being owned as a slave)
Cow wha belang a butcher neber sey him bery-well.
(A cow that belongs to a butcher never says 'I'm very well.')

'Good bwoy' a nickname fi fool.
('Good boy' is a fool's nickname.)

(On being disadvantaged)
Him a cleber man wha dribe way hungry just workin him jaw.
(He is a clever man who drives away hunger by just working his jaws.)

When dog wake a marnin him praya sey,
'Teday—eider blow or bone!'
(When the dog gets up each morning its prayer says,
'Again today, a blow or a bone!')

Dog sey, befoh him plant yam fi look like maskita foot,
him satisfy fi tun begga.
(The dog says that instead of planting yams to look
like mosquito legs, he prefers to become a beggar.)

Hungry-Belly and Full-Belly noh walk same pass.
(The rich and the poor do not meet.)

Call tiger 'Massa' him still nyam yu.
(Call a tiger 'Master' he'll still eat you.)

(*On feeling hardships are unfair*)
Jackass sey de worl noh leble.
(The donkey says the world isn't level ground.)

Racktone a riber-battam nah know sun-hot.
(A stone at the bottom of the river doesn't know the heat of the sun.)

Wahn lib a wuk—awks neyga baby!
(You want to live at work—ask the black person's baby.)

(*On scapegoating*)
Cos parrot noisy-noisy, dem sey a dem one nyam up banana.
(Because parrots are chatterers people say they are the only ones who eat up the fruits.)

(*On how when somebody gets bad treatment you too could get the same*)
De tick wha flog de black dog wi whip de white.
(The same stick that flogs the black dog will also flog the white one.)

(*On contradictions*)
Needle mek clothes, but needle himself naked.
(The needle makes clothes yet the needle itself is naked.)

(*On relying on your own initiative*)
Noh wait till drum beat befoh yu grine yu axe.
(Don't wait till you hear the drum beat before you grind your axe.)

Yu cahn stap bud fram a-fly ober yu, but yu can stap him a-mek nes pon tap a yu head.
(You can't stop a bird from flying over you, but you can stop it from making a nest on top of your head.)

(On support)

If yu back monkey him wi fight tiger.
(If you back a monkey he'll fight a tiger.)

(On being thrifty)

Mista Manage-Good betta dan Mista Big Wage.
(Mister Manage-Well will find he's better off than Mister Big-Wage
and bad management.)

(On the way an angry noise can be a useless threat)

Dog-bark neber frightn moon!
(A dog's bark isn't going to frighten the moon.)

Jamaican Song

Little toad little toad mind yourself
mind yourself let me plant my corn
plant my corn to feed my horse
feed my horse to run my race—
the sea is full of more than I know
moon is bright like night time sun
night is dark like all eyes shut
    Mind—mind yu not harmed
    somody know bout yu
    somody know bout yu

Little toad little toad mind yourself
mind yourself let me build my house
build my house to be at home
be at home till I one day vanish—
the sea is full of more than I know
moon is bright like night time sun
night is dark like all eyes shut
    Mind—mind yu not harmed
    somody know bout yu
    somody know bout yu

Mek Drum Talk, Man

for Caribbean Independence

Budoom-a budoom-a budoom-a ba-dap.
A-dudu-wum a-dudu-wum dudu-wum a-dudu-wum.
Wake skin up. Wake skin.
Slap it up. Slap skin.
Man, slap up drum.
Use yu hundred han them.
Domination get drop.
Some doors get open up.

    Lawks O, slap the drum, slap it Buddy.
    Slap it like yu a mad mad somody—
    budoom-a budoom-a budoom-a ba-dap,
    budoom-a budoom-a budoom-a ba-dap.
    A-dudu-wum a-dudu-wum dudu-wum a-dudu-wum.
    Budoom-a dudu-wum. Budoom-a dudu-wum. Bru-dum.

Let out lost ancestor voice.
Let out of skin all pain and vice.
Tell the worl that the king is dead—
forbidden people gettn wed.
Tell towns new words comin fo print—
knowledge looked-fo whe palms they skint.
Get soun like them a talkin gong,
mek them happy jus a-galang.

Get the soun, get the soun, get it Buddy.
Wake up gong and family.
Every soun is head with a hum
of deep-deep voice of drum—
tru the windows, tru the trees,
tru the markets, tru the streets.

    Lawks O, slap the drum, slap it Buddy.
    Slap it like yu a mad mad somody—
    budoom-a budoom-a budoom-a ba-dap,
    budoom-a budoom-a budoom-a ba-dap.
    A-dudu-wum a-dudu-wum dudu-wum a-dudu-wum.
    Budoom-a dudu-wum. Budoom-a dudu-wum. Bru-dum.

Slap the drum. Elbow drum. Thump drum.
Mek drum sey to be hit is fun.
Wake up skin. Wake up skin
with it broom bu-doom it hidin.
People cry—start a new cycle!
Widen money circle!
Get out every hiddn moan.
Let loose all skin-hiddn groan.

Show off the pulse of big bright sun.
Sen good news to village and town.
Tell the people a child is born,
tell them about a sweet new dawn.
Bring street drummin in the house—
see sleepers get aroused.
Wake the people out-a they trance.
Tell people come dance.

    Lawks O, slap the drum, slap it Buddy.
    Slap it like yu a mad mad somody—
    budoom-a budoom-a budoom-a ba-dap,
    budoom-a budoom-a budoom-a ba-dap.
    A-dudu-wum a-dudu-wum dudu-wum a-dudu-wum.
    Budoom-a dudu-wum. Budoom-a dudu-wum. Bru-dum.

a-galang—going along
somody—somebody

Bye Now

Walk good
Walk good
Noh mek macca go juk yu
Or cow go buck yu.
Noh mek dog bite yu
Or hungry go ketch yu , yah!

Noh mek sunhot turn yu dry.
Noh mek rain soak yu.
Noh mek tief tief yu
Or stone go buck yu foot, yah!
Walk good
Walk good

Goodbye Now

Walk well
Walk well
Don't let thorns run in you
Or let a cow butt you.
Don't let a dog bite you
Or hunger catch you, hear!

Don't let sun's heat turn you dry.
Don't let rain soak you.
Don't let a thief rob you
Or a stone bump your foot, hear!
Walk well
Walk well

Pods Pop and Grin

Pods Pop and Grin

Strong strong sun, in that look
you have, lands ripen
fruits, trees, people.

Lands love the flame of your gaze.
Lands hide some warmth
of sun-eye for darkness.

All for you pods pop and grin.
Bananas hurry up and grow.
Coconut becomes water and oil.

Palm trees try to fly to you
but just dance everywhere.
Silk leaves of bamboo rustle wild.

And when rain finished falling
winds shake diamonds from branches
that again feel your eye.

Strong strong sun, in you
lands keep ripening
fruits, trees, people.

Birds go on tuning up
and don't care at all—
more blood berries are coming.

Your look strokes up all
summertime. We hear streams running.
You come back every day.

Hurricane

Under low black clouds
the wind was all
speedy feet, all horns and breath,
all bangs, howls, rattles,
in every hen house,
church hall and school.

Roaring, screaming, returning,
it made forced entry, shoved walls,
made rifts, brought roofs down,
hitting rooms to sticks apart.

It wrung soft banana trees,
broke tough trunks of palms.
It pounded vines of yams,
left fields battered up.

Invisible with such ecstasy—
with no intervention of sun or man—
everywhere kept changing branches.

Zinc sheets are kites.
Leaves are panic swarms.
Fowls are fixed with feathers turned.
Goats, dogs, pigs,
all are people together.

Then growling it slunk away
from muddy, mossy trail and boats
in hedges: and cows, ratbats, trees,
fish, all dead in the road.

Workings of the Wind

Wind doesn't always topple trees
and shake houses to pieces.

> Wind plays
> all over woods, with weighty ghosts
> in swings in thousands,
> swinging from every branch.

Wind doesn't always rattle windows
and push, push at walls.

> Wind whistles
> down cul-de-sacs and worries
> dry leaves and old newspapers to leap
> and curl like kite tails.

Wind doesn't always dry out
sweaty shirts and blouses.

> Wind scatters
> pollen dust of flowers, washes
> people's and animals' faces
> and combs out birds' feathers.

Wind doesn't always whip up waves
into white horses.

> Wind shakes up
> tree-shadows to dance on rivers,
> to jig about on grass, and hanging
> lantern light to play signalman.

Wind doesn't always run wild
kicking tinny dustbin lids.

> Wind makes
> leafy limbs bow to red roses
> and bob up and down outside windows
> and makes desk papers fly up indoors.

Banana Talk

Shoot of a soft heart pushes:
we go pendulous
and it's all
SUN'S persuasion
in the growing baby of a bunch.

Flapped round by long leaves
feather shaped, in wind's coos
and whistles, and stuffed up
with great SUN and simple rain,
we become full, curved by closeness.

And where intangible spices come solid
is where SUN works long hours
and SUN'S fingers become bananas.

Rooted randomly together
in backyard's kitchen care
we bananas go bountiful.

In fields all poverty worn
we linger a lot
but we seldom give up.

In big walks handing out
all packed food messages,
all packed clean living,
we hurry and get full
but we will be cuddle curved.

And peeled, exposed a banana,
sensations of SUN hit tongues
with flowers and cinnamon.

And banana yellowgold, excluded
for only men, makes men bury bananas
from rats, birds and creepy crawlies
in lonely bushy places.

And in our sunny yellow or green
we love to go and excite
market places, among other
SUN coloured fruit
and vivid talk and people.

And we bananas curl with apples.
We stand beside tomatoes.
We help a plain bowl serve colours.
We move eyes and lips.
Hands go for hands of bananas.

Light Fabric

Oranges the tree hung around itself
while people were asleep
are miniature suns in their bowl.

Bananas curled in words at the table
are only other spices of land
that came ripe through the door

The apples piled nought-shaped
are other mixes too April made
and September cupped colourfully

Distinguished writer and poet James Berry was born and raised in Jamaica, and he presently lives in England. He has published poems and short stories in the Caribbean, Great Britain, and the United States. His short-story collection, *A Thief in the Village,* was a 1989 Coretta Scott King Honor Book. *When I Dance* is his first book of poetry specifically written for young people.

In 1990, James Berry received the Order of the British Empire in recognition of his great contribution to people of all ages through his writing.